COYOTE PETERSON

WILDLIFE ADVENTURE

AN INTERACTIVE GUIDE WITH FACTS, PHOTOS, AND MORE!

Little, Brown and Company
New York Boston

Sometimes the journeys we take in life are more about the adventure than the accomplishment.

—Coyote Peterson

Hi,
I'm Coyote Peterson,
and I *love* animals.

I film wildlife encounters with my Brave Wilderness crew in amazing places around the world. But when I was growing up, my first wildlife adventures began in my backyard in Newbury, Ohio. Your backyard, front yard, or local park are the perfect places to start your own adventures, too! There are countless animals and insects making their homes in each unique environment. To get started, you just have to observe, identify, and record your findings as you take in your surroundings.

When I hit the trail, I take my journal with me. Recording my wildlife observations—from catching common snapping turtles in Ohio to coming face-to-snout with a wolverine in Alaska—is a great way to keep track of the environments I explore as well as all the animals I've been lucky enough to encounter!

I'm glad I have my journals—and my photos and videos—as proof! But you don't need to be in an exotic place to explore. Examining life in your backyard gives you the chance to learn more about a species that you probably come across almost every day.

PORCUPINE

EUROPEAN HONEY BEE

Don't forget to sketch! Sketching an animal or its habitat will allow you to see them in a whole new way!

Get outside! Be brave, but also be aware. Explore as if you are a wilderness detective, using all your senses to learn everything you can about your surroundings. What do you smell? How does it feel? Is it hot or cold? Is it humid or dry? These are all important things when learning about an animal's habitat.

Observation is key when it comes to wilderness adventures. When you encounter animals in their habitats, you want to be able to notice key characteristics that make one individual different from the next. For example: Observation and patience will eventually lead to the ability to distinguish subtle size and coloration differences between two snakes, which is very important for identifying which one is venomous!

When I wasn't in my backyard as a kid, I would be at the library, scouring books for information on creatures I'd never seen. If you love animals the way I do, then you probably spend just as much time reading about them as you do searching for them, too. Reading about animals taught me the correct biological and zoological terms used in the field. For example, before working with snapping turtles, I learned the difference between a "plastron" and "carapace."

Plastron

In every episode of my show, I tell the Coyote Pack to "Be Brave" and "Stay Wild." These words are to encourage you to seek out new experiences bravely, expand your boundaries, and explore the wild, natural world around you. But being brave doesn't mean taking risks! Always respect the dangers of your environment and develop the skills it takes to safely navigate your interactions with wildlife.

Carapace

Over time, you'll feel more comfortable and courageous when faced with new challenges, and you'll have the knowledge and ability to overcome them.

EXPLORE YOUR BACKYARD!

You don't need super-cool gear to get started. An old plastic container with holes punched in the lid is a great way to collect small species like insects and amphibians. Talk to an adult before you make a critter container, and definitely don't take any tweezers or salad tongs without asking! In the summer, always make sure you wear sunscreen and have drinking water available. Safety first!

Before you go into your yard with your gear and tools:

1 Write down three things you expect to see. For example: What species do you expect to see? What might it look like? Where does it live?

_____

_____

_____

2 Once you are outside, observe what is different from what you expected. Did you discover something new?

_____

_____

_____

3 Draw your favorite backyard animal or take notes about something new you observed.

Now that you've explored your backyard, it's time to learn some wilderness vocabulary. Here's a crossword with some words you'll hear me say on my show... and maybe even see in this guide.

Use these words to finish the crossword:

APEX
APOSEMATIC
ARBOREAL
BIODIVERSITY
CAMOUFLAGE
CONSERVATION
ECOSYSTEM
EXOSKELETON
INVASIVE
NOCTURAL
OCEANS
OPPORTUNISTIC
PREDATOR
VENOM

ACROSS

2. Animals that are active at night are_____, whereas animals that are active during the day are diurnal

4. A word for a plant or animal that invades and dominates a new habitat

5. An animal that hunts other animals as a source of food

7. Bright, contrasting coloration or markings, serving to warn or repel predators

9. Taking advantage of a situation—for example, when an animal eats whatever is available

11. An external covering that protects an animal's body. HINT: crabs and insects

13. The top or highest part of something

14. A community of organisms and their environment

DOWN:

1. The act of taking care of an animal or habitat, trying to protect it for the future

3. Animals that are _____ live most of their lives in trees

6. Using color, patterns, or markings as a disguise in one's environment

8. The variety of life—plants and animals—in a particular place

10. A toxic substance produced by some animals that is injected into a victim by biting or stinging

12. The most unexplored places on the planet

CREEKS

Scientists use a naming system called *taxonomy* to classify biodiversity. This system divides animals into groups based on similar characteristics. Examples of these groups include mammals, amphibians, and insects.

At an early age, I discovered the amazing display of biodiversity that can be found in freshwater creeks. If you've watched any of the Brave Wilderness videos, you've witnessed my love for scrambling along a creek bed, flipping over rocks to see what interesting creatures may be hiding underneath. Freshwater, sandy pockets, and smooth rocks are just some of the characteristics that define this ecosystem, allowing a wide range of animals to thrive.

Here are some examples of the fascinating species who call these flowing waterways home:

Mammals: Raccoons, Gray squirrels, Minks
Reptiles: Wood turtles, Eastern painted turtles, Water snakes, Garter snakes
Birds: Mallard ducks, Robins, Cardinals, Kingfishers
Fish: Bluegill, Mosquitofish, Minnows
Insects: Water striders, Mayflies, Dragonflies
Arachnids: Orb weavers, Wolf spiders
Crustacean: Crayfish, Blue crayfish
Amphibians: American toads, Red-spotted newts, Eastern hellbenders, Dusky salamanders

Orb weaver

Red-eared slider

OUCH! Crayfish pinch me every time!

Crayfish

Water snake

Eastern tiger swallowtail

Painted turtles are the most widespread turtles native to North America, ranging from the Atlantic to the Pacific and from Canada to Mexico.

Eastern hellbender salamander

To track down some of these creek critters, you'll need:

- Dip net
- Water shoes or rubber boots
- Plastic critter containers
- Magnifying glass
- Bucket

The Incredibly COOL Blue Crayfish!

Five fun facts!

1 They crawl forward, but swim backward!

2 They are related to lobsters.

3 They can lose their claws and regrow (or *regenerate*) them.

4 Blue crayfish are subterranean, which means they live underground and burrow holes up to eight feet deep!

5 Their eyes are attached to the end of moveable stalks.

Crustacean Crawl

Follow this blue crayfish along its path to find its burrow:

FUN FACTS!

Crayfish have gills to breathe underwater, but they can also breathe out of water as long as their gills stay wet. In a humid (damp) environment, they can breathe out of water for months!

START

Metamorphosis

Check out these diagrams of the metamorphosis of a frog!
Can you put the stages in the correct order?

A. _____

B. _____

C. _____

D. _____

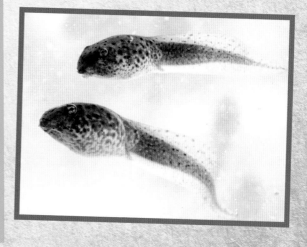

E. _____

Cool, clear water tumbles over moss-covered rocks across the forest floor. Fish gather in calm secluded pools, and the shores of the creek bed are alive with a chorus of buzzes, splashes, and the croaking of frogs. It's time to turn over rocks, peek into tree hollows, and plunge your hand into the chilly water to uncover some creek-side creatures!

TEMPERATE FORESTS

Temperate forests, like the vast wilderness of Alaska, see the widest seasonal changes. Nevertheless, both the plants and animals that live here exhibit incredible resilience with their ability to withstand these environmental cycles. The landscape changes dramatically from a dense green woodland—capable of hiding some of the largest roaming animals—to an icy frontier with bare trees and deep snow. As the temperatures drop and the green grasses dry out, many mammals adjust to the coming winter by growing thicker fur coats and fat reserves, while some prepare for hibernation, a sleep-like state that includes a reduced heart rate, breathing, and body temperature that can last for months.

It's during the warmer summer months that you will find these animals more active, because it's when an abundance of food is available.

Let's take a look at some of the creatures we might find in the temperate forests of North America:

Mammals: Mule deer, Moose, Red foxes, Black bears, Elk, Wolverines, Porcupines, Grizzly bears, Pine martens, Lynx

Birds: Red-tailed hawks, Bald eagles, Golden eagles, Pileated woodpeckers, Great horned owls, Steller's jays

Fox

Yikes! Look at those teeth! Grizzly bears have super-strong jaws, with a bite force of up to 1,200 psi!* A human's bite is only about 175 psi—what a difference!

Grizzy bear

*pounds per square inch

This adorable black bear cub is shedding its winter coat. You can see the thicker fur still remaining down the center of its back.

Black bear

Lynx

Porcupine

Bald eagle

Gotta-have Gear for Forest Outings:

- Walking stick
- Binoculars
- Backpack
- Animal tracks field guide
- Hiking boots
- Gloves, hat, and scarf for winter outings!

Karen
the Moose

MWAH!

Of course, I would never smooch a *wild* moose! Karen is an orphaned calf who had been raised in captivity at a local wildlife sanctuary. Some animals are too dangerous to have encounters with in the wild, so we work with conservationists to feature ambassador animals living in these sanctuaries to help us raise awareness for the needs of their wild cousins and the habitats in which they live.

Working with animals in captivity has given us several unforgettable encounters, including fulfilling my childhood dream of meeting a wolverine, and even climbing a tree after an adorable pine marten.

Wolverine

Pine marten

The wolverine and the pine marten are incredibly successful predators. They are both mammals who live in northern temperate forests. But what else do they have in common? Are you a wiz when it comes to wolverines? A master of pine martens? Take the quiz to find out!

Wolverine vs. Pine Marten

Read the fascinating facts below, and determine if it refers to the *wolverine*, the *pine marten*, or *both* by placing the activity stickers in the correct circles!

A mustelid, which means it is a member of the weasel family.

Coyote has a plush version of this animal that his mom made for him when he was a kid.

Is arboreal, which means it spends most of its time in trees.

Has a light bib of dark-yellow to white fur on its chest and throat.

Can kill prey much larger than its size, such as elk.

Has several natural enemies, such as owls, bobcats, coyotes, and wolves.

Although it's a predator, it's also an omnivore, eating both meat and plant material.

More active in the summer than in the winter, but does not hibernate.

As you walk through a temperate forest, listen for the sounds of wildlife: bark being chipped, the shrill call of a hawk, or a big lumbering giant moving in the distance. Thin beams of sunlight dance through the gaps in the leaves, making it difficult to spot stealthy animals. Keep an eye on the ground for animal tracks, and have your binoculars handy, because the woods are full of wonder!

SONORAN DESERT

The sandy, dry earth and spiky vegetation make the desert seem like a desolate, lifeless place, but it is actually a rich habitat with tons of fascinating creatures. Ever since I was a kid, one of my favorite places to explore has been the Sonoran Desert. With saguaro, prickly pears, and cholla cacti scattered across the landscape, and huge mountains on the horizon, this unique landscape is home to many extraordinary, specialized creatures. Walking along a dried-up desert wash, I've seen over ten species in just an hour's time! Desert creatures have outstanding camouflage, killer venom, vivid coloration, and survival instincts adapted to harsh conditions. Many of them appear early in the morning and seek shade or burrow underground in the hot afternoon. Others avoid the scorching sun altogether and only emerge at night. Despite the infrequent rains, blistering heat, and dry winds, the desert hosts an incredible variety of life.

Here are some of our favorite desert-dwelling species:

Mammals: Coyotes, Desert pocket mice, Kangaroo rats, Mexican free-tailed bats, Kit foxes

Reptiles: Western diamondback rattlesnakes, Arizona coral snakes, Arizona mountain kingsnakes, Regal horned lizards, Gila monsters, Western banded geckos, Desert tortoises

Birds: Roadrunners, Gilded flickers, Elf owls

Anthropods: Giant desert centipedes

Arachnids: Giant desert hairy scorpions, Desert blonde tarantulas

A saguaro is a tall cactus with branches shaped like a candelabra.

Giant desert centipede

Giant desert centipedes are voracious predators, hunting lizards, rodents, birds, and even snakes!

Although the western diamondback is the largest rattlesnake in the Southwestern US, the Mojave rattlesnake—which has very similar patterning—boasts venom that is considered to be the most potent of all rattlesnakes. Luckily, prompt medical attention allows for a very high survival rate.

Western diamondback rattlesnake

DID YOU KNOW?
Did you know that a rattlesnake can shake its rattle back and forth more than sixty times per second?!

The Gila monster is the only venomous lizard in the United States!

Gila monster

Because desert conditions can be brutal, you need extra protection during the day, and alternate gear for nighttime exploration.

Desert blonde tarantula

Gear You'll Need for the Desert:
- Hat with large rim for shade
- Bandana
- Water bottle
- Flashlight
- Plastic critter containers
- Insect net
- Pants and long sleeves
- UV light for scorpions
- Hiking boots

Creatures of the Heat!

Arizona coral snake

Arizona mountain kingsnake

Watch out! Be sure not to mistake an Arizona coral snake for an Arizona mountain kingsnake! Coral snakes typically have red, black, and yellow stripes, and are highly venomous. Arizona mountain kingsnakes have red, black, and cream stripes—instead of yellow—resembling Arizona coral snakes. Take extra precautions, because although one is harmless, the other can be deadly!

Am I Nocturnal or Diurnal?

Write *"Nocturnal"* for creatures that come out at night, or *"Diurnal"* for creatures seen in the daytime, or *"Both"*!

_____ **KIT FOX**

_____ **TARANTULA HAWK**

_____ **BANDED GECKO**

_____ **ELF OWL**

_____ **COLLARED LIZARD**

_____ **GILA MONSTER**

_____ **COYOTE**

_____ **ROADRUNNER**

_____ **KANGAROO RAT**

_____ **MEXICAN FREE-TAILED BAT**

Make a Match

Place the correct desert animal sticker with its name.
Can you match them all without looking them up? Do your best!

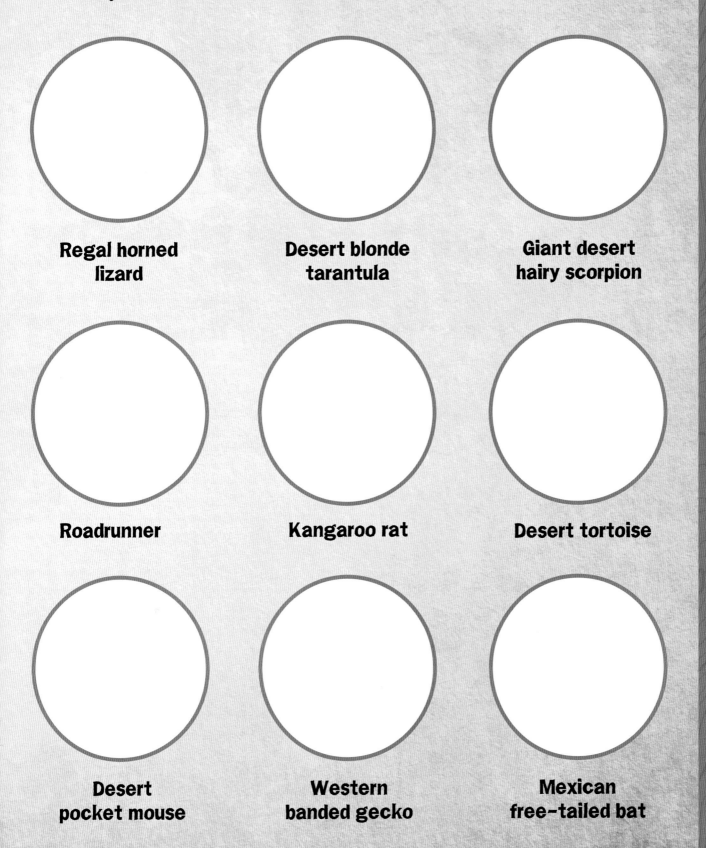

**Regal horned
lizard**

**Desert blonde
tarantula**

**Giant desert
hairy scorpion**

Roadrunner

Kangaroo rat

Desert tortoise

**Desert
pocket mouse**

**Western
banded gecko**

**Mexican
free-tailed bat**

When the sun is high in the sky, it's the ideal time to look for diurnal creatures in the desert, since most will head for shade as temperatures soar up to 110° F. You might see birds nesting in the tall saguaro cactus, or wasps on the flowers of the prickly pear. But watch your step! The desert is also home to many venomous reptiles and insects!

SWAMPS

When I think about the numerous types of swamplands, I also think about the diversity of bizarre and elusive creatures who thrive in the murky waters and thick, boot-sticking muck. While there are plenty of docile species, many of them are ferocious predators, requiring an extra level of caution.

Wading through the murky water can be a dangerous game, as you never know what may be slithering past your feet. The swamplands of the southeastern United States are home to venomous snakes, huge crocodilians, and needle-toothed fish, not to mention my personal favorite, snapping turtles!

Here are just a few of the amazing animals you might find:

Mammals: Opossums, Beavers, Muskrats
Reptiles: Alligator snapping turtles, Banded water snakes, American alligators, Water moccasins, Common snapping turtles
Amphibians: American bullfrogs, Leopard frogs
Birds: Great blue herons, Green herons, Barred owls, Wood ducks
Insect: Toe-biters (giant water bug)
Fish: Snakehead fish, Spotted gars

Common snapping turtle

Banded water snake

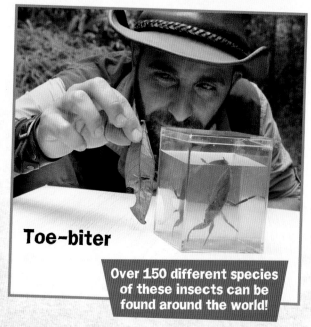

Toe-biter

Over 150 different species of these insects can be found around the world!

Alligator snapping turtle

Alligator snapping turtles have a more distinct hooked beak, much spikier shell, and can weigh almost three times as much as their "common" cousins.

Spotted gar

American bullfrog

Male bullfrogs can be distinguished by their yellow throats.

Barred owl

Whether in a kayak, airboat, or on your own two feet, you've got to pack the right gear:

- Waders or rubber boots
- Large dip net
- Plastic critter containers
- Snake hook or tongs
- Bug spray
- Bucket

Mighty SNAPPER Features!

Few predators are better evolved for their environment than the fierce common snapping turtle. Let's take a look at how their special characteristics make them the rulers of the wetland:

A pointed beak to latch on to prey

A shell sometimes covered in algae for stealthy hunting

Long, strong claws for digging and defense

A long tail with a ridge of pointed, bony scales

A long muscular neck for a super-fast strike

Bone-crushing jaws with scissor power

A Quiz! Oh Snap!

What do you really know about the common snapping turtle? Circle all the correct answers.

1 What is a defense mechanism for snapping turtles?

Hiding in the Mud!   Venomous Stinger!   Stinky musk!   Aggressive chomp!

2 Snapping turtles can pull their heads and legs into their shells!

True!   False!

3 Why do snapping turtles fight each other?

For territory!   For practice!   For mates!   For fun!   For food!

4 Sometimes snapping turtles go on land to:

Bask in the sun!   Lay eggs!   Go for a walk!   Eat grass!   Find another pond!

Fascinating Facts!

Use the word bank to fill in the blanks!

American alligators are ferocious ambush _____, which means they use stealth and patience when hunting. Many different animals are on the menu, including birds, _____, _____, turtles, and snakes. With a bite force of nearly 2,000 psi, large adult alligators can even crack through an average-size snapping turtle's shell! Alligators can have up to eighty _____ at a time, and constantly _____ them as they wear down or fall out.

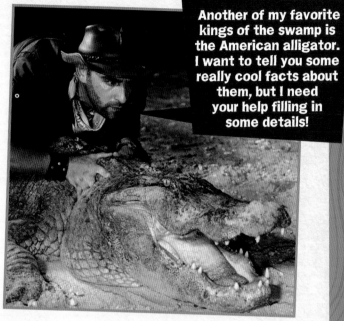

Another of my favorite kings of the swamp is the American alligator. I want to tell you some really cool facts about them, but I need your help filling in some details!

Alligators are mostly _____ creatures and can hold their breath for around fifteen minutes at a time. Their _____ are situated on the tops of their snouts, so as they silently hunt on the surface of the water while partially submerged, they can still breathe. When they find their prey, their powerful _____ propel them through the water at up to _____ MPH!

Alligators are amazing mothers! They can have up to fifty _____ at a time and will look after the hatchlings for the first one to _____ years of their lives! When their babies hatch, they are like mini adults and are born with a full set of teeth. They will reach full size in about ten _____. A wild adult male alligator can grow up to _____ feet long and weigh up to 1,000 _____!

WORD BANK

AQUATIC	MAMMALS	REGENERATE	TWENTY
EGGS	NOSTRILS	TAILS	YEARS
FIFTEEN	POUNDS	TEETH	
FISH	PREDATORS	THREE	

Prepare to get muddy exploring the murky muck of the swamp! Look closely at the surface of the water—you might see the top of an alligator or the shell of a turtle. During the day, many animals will seek shelter in thick, tall marsh grasses, under logs, or in the cloudy water to avoid the scorching sun. Watch where you step— dangerous camouflaged creatures are everywhere!

INTERTIDAL POOLS

When I explored the tide pools and shallow reefs of Hawaii, I was amazed. From docile sea cucumbers to the venomous crown-of-thorns sea stars, the warm shallow waters hosted an amazing array of life.

Whether searching in the isolated, rocky tide pools, or venturing out into the shallow coastal waters, starting your adventure at low tide is the best time to observe a variety of marine life. But watch out! Tide pool creatures can be venomous and even deadly! Always make sure you have a field guide to help you identify what creatures can be handled and which to observe from a safe distance. Remember—*if you don't know what it is, don't touch it!*

Here are fabulous finds in a Pacific Island tide pool or coral reef:

Reptiles: Yellow-bellied sea snakes
Birds: Albatrosses, Petrels, Terns
Fish: Scorpionfish, Moray eels, Bluelined surgeonfish, Zebra blennies
Mollusk: Day octopus, Textile cone snails
Crustacean: Ghost crabs, Hermit crabs
Echinoderms: Red slate pencil urchins, Sea cucumbers, Crown-of-thorns sea stars

Yellow-bellied sea snake

DID YOU KNOW?

Because this snake lives its entire life in the water, it has adapted the ability to absorb oxygen through its skin!

Red slate pencil urchin

Ghost crab

ALWAYS identify a species before handling it! Many marine creatures, like the Crown-of-thorns sea star, are covered in venomous spikes.

Crown-of-thorns

DID YOU KNOW?

These blue-lined beauties have defensive spines on their tails that are as sharp as a scalpel. That's why they're called surgeonfish!

Blue-lined surgeonfish

Day octopus

Warty sea cucumber

Gear and Tools for an Outing in the Tide Pools:

- Mask and snorkel
- Water shoes
- Dip net
- Field guide
- Sunscreen

The DEADLIEST Dangers!

Can you identify the animals using the hints below? Place the correct animal sticker next to the circle, and then number them in order from 1 to 9, with 9 being the deadliest and most dangerous!

I live in many places around the world. I have ten legs, two of which are tipped with pinchers. Because I eat toxic stuff on the beach, I can make you sick if you eat me. ___

Despite my spines, I have no backbone. I can have ten to twenty arms, and grow up to three feet across. To eat coral, I ooze my stomach out of my mouth and onto my prey, slowly digesting it. Watch out! My spines are venomous! ___

I am black and bright yellow, with an oarlike tail. My venom is extremely toxic to humans, but I rarely see them because I prefer to live in deep water. ___

I often hide in narrow rock crevices in warm water, allowing only my head to peek out. I have long, sharp teeth in my mouth, and even more teeth in my throat! I'm not venomous, but I still have an aggressive, painful bite. ___

I come in many colors and shapes, and love warm coastal waters. I filter sand through my body like an earthworm, eating plant matter and algae. There are 1,200 species of me found all over the world! ___

I am slow and stick to the bottom of shallow waters. I have sharp spines all over my body like a pincushion. If you step on my venom-laced spines, they will break off in your foot. Though they're not deadly, you'll need tweezers to get them out!

Named for the stinging barbs concealed in my dorsal fin, I blend in perfectly to the bottom of shallow water, so be careful where you walk. My spines are venomous and painful, but not as potent as my cousin the stonefish!

Although my shell is beautiful, I am a fierce predator. I move slowly along the bottom of my watery home, where I catch fish. I hunt with a harpoon-like tooth and inject highly toxic and immobilizing venom into my prey. Anyone stung by me must seek medical attention.

I may be small, delicate, and not as potent as my Australian cousins, but my tendrils are laced with venom. People avoid swimming during the full moon, because that's often when I come close to shore.

If you don't recognize a species, it is always a case of "Look, but don't touch." My crew and I are professionally trained, and we *still* use field guides to identify unknown species!

Hawaii is a chain of volcanic islands in the middle of the Pacific Ocean. Eight main islands make up seven hundred fifty miles of coastline. The archipelago has five active volcanos, and as they erupt, the land literally grows out of the ocean! Because Hawaii did not break off from a continent, there are several species that can be found only in this unique ecosystem. The rough volcanic rock provides nutrients for marine plants and coral, and plenty of cover and places to hide, making Hawaii's tide pools rich with life.

OCEANS

Oceans are the vastest and most unexplored ecosystems on Earth. The Atlantic, the world's second-largest ocean, is home to an incredible array of life, including thousands of fish species that can't be found anywhere else! That's why the Brave Wilderness crew and I decided to become fully certified divers. We were ready for new adventures! Whether we are swimming with sharks, playing with dolphins, or exploring reefs, witnessing the diverse marine life and rich ecosystems remind us that our oceans are truly magnificent.

It would be impossible to pick a favorite, but some of the amazing creatures we've encountered so far are:

Mammals: Spotted dolphins, Baleen whales, Orcas, Right whales

Birds: Brown pelicans, Magnificent frigatebirds, Cormorants, Cory's shearwaters

Fish: Tiger sharks, Marlins, Angelfish Reef sharks, Sardines, Bluefin tunas, Hammerhead sharks, Remoras

Mollusks: Conchs, Brief squids

Tiger shark

Magnificent frigatebird

Brown pelican

DID YOU KNOW?

The magnificent frigatebird typically catches fish while in flight as they jump from the water, but it will also bully other birds to regurgitate food for them.

Hammerhead shark

Brief squid

Humpback
whale

DID YOU KNOW?

Humpback whales are a species
of baleen whale! *Baleen* refers
to their comblike teeth, which
capture small prey as they
move through the water!

Spotted dolphin

**Gear you will need for
an aquatic adventure:**

- Dive mask, snorkel, and fins
- Wet suit
- Underwater housing for camera
- Dive gear: buoyancy compensator
  device (BCD), regulators, dive
  computer, tanks *
* Scuba diving requires certification

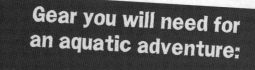

What do spotted dolphins, tiger sharks, cormorants, and marlin have in common? They will all feast together on a school of sardines! When a school is detected, it slowly attracts a host of hungry hunters. The predators do not contend with one another, but instead surround the school and attack it from all sides, taking advantage of the bait ball.

Find the stickers to finish the picture of this feast!

Place the animals around the school as they take their part in a fish feeding frenzy!

Cormorants dive straight down from above.

...otted dolphins work ...ether to break into ... swarm of sardines ...nd keep them at the surface.

An enormous baleen whale might swoop in at the end for one

...rlin and bluefin tuna ...tack from below

SUPER Creature Feature

One of our most awesome aquatic experiences was swimming with a very bold hammerhead shark in the Bahamas. Its distinct head shape is a unique adaptation that is advantageous when catching its favorite food: stingrays!

The eye placement on the far sides of its face helps it search a greater area.

Its long, flat, strong head allows it to pin prey against the ocean floor.

Its face has special sensors that help detect prey.

Hunt for Prey

Can you find the path that leads this hammerhead shark to its favorite food?

START

END

The crystal—clear tropical waters of the Atlantic Ocean are like a giant aquarium. Birds fly overhead looking for an easy catch, while below, a flurry of fins and flippers scour the reefs and rocks for food. Although it may be an alien world to humans, the ocean is home to around 80 percent of all life on Earth!

RAIN FORESTS

COSTA RICA

The rain forest is everything I've ever imagined. Standing in the humid Costa Rican jungle, you'll note a wide variety of sounds: the buzzing of insects, the chirping of songbirds, and the slither of creatures through the thick leaf litter of the forest floor. Then you'll notice vines reaching high up from the shaded forest floor into the dense leaves of the canopy. Dotting the blankets of lush greens are the bright colors of poison dart frogs and eyelash vipers. But not all threats warn you with aposematic coloration. Other toxic creatures include wandering spiders and scorpions.

Many of the rain forest's animals can be dangerous, so be sure to keep your distance until you can accurately identify them:

Mammals: Capuchin monkeys, Two-toed sloths, Ocelots
Reptiles: Fer-de-lance vipers, Green basilisk lizards, Eyelash vipers, Boa constrictors, Parrot snakes
Birds: Scarlet macaws, Keel-billed toucans
Insects: Blue morpho butterflies, Leaf mantises
Arachnids: Wandering spiders, Bark scorpions
Amphibians: Poison dart frogs, Tree frogs, Glass frogs

Leaf mantis

Red-eyed tree frog

Granular poison frog

This frog's aposematic coloration warns predators of its toxicity!

Golden eyelash viper

Ocelot

I'm lucky this was only a juvenile or else our interaction might not have been as playful!

Toucan

DID YOU KNOW?

Because of their big bills, toucans can't fly for very long. Instead, they use their curved toes and claws to hop between tree branches!

Wandering spider

I'd never try to free handle this guy. If I were bitten, with its neurotoxic venom, I'd be on my way to the hospital!

Gear and Tools You Will Need for a Rain Forest Adventure:

- Snake hook and snake tongs
- Plastic critter containers
- Boots
- Binoculars
- Bug net
- Hat
- Bandana
- Water bottle
- Backpack

The rain forest has life at all levels.

Rising 100 to 150 feet, the top level is called the canopy. There, the sun drenches the highest branches with light. The very top is home to butterflies, bats, and birds of prey. A little lower, under the roof of thick leaves, you will find monkeys, sloths, a few insects, and smaller tropical birds.

The middle level is the understory, which starts at about fifty feet and goes down to the forest floor. Most of the sunlight is blocked by the canopy, so the plants that grow here have large, broad leaves. Flying insects and arboreal ants (like the bullet ant) forage in this layer, as well as birds, butterflies, arboreal snakes, lizards, and tree frogs.

The bottom level is called the forest floor. The floor is dark, hot, and humid because of the moist air trapped by the growth of the understory. Multitudes of crawling insects live here, as well as venomous snakes, spiders, frogs, and the iconic ocelot.

FOREST FLOOR

Who Lives Where?

Find the stickers and place each species at the level that it calls home.

Fer-de-lance viper

Golden eyelash viper

Scarlet macaw

Capuchin monkey

Two-toed sloth

Red-eyed tree frog

Green-and-black poison dart frog

Green basilisk lizard

Bullet ant

Blue morpho butterfly

Leaf mantis

Wandering spider

Ocelot

Boa constrictor

Toucan

Python millipede

The rain forest is the richest ecosystem in the world, humming with constant activity day and night. Check under the broad, moisture-soaked leaves for frog eggs, and on the wide tree trunks for lizards and insects. The camouflaged patterns and brilliant hues of the rain forest and its animals are a spectacle! Keep your eyes open, and you're sure to find some colorful creatures!

THE AFRICAN SAVANNA

A savanna is a plain characterized by course grasses and scattered trees. Most are located close to the equator, so extreme heat is very common. The animals who live here are true survivors. Every day is a battle to find food—and not become food!

However, the eastern savannas of South Africa enjoy more rainfall since they are closer to the coast. This allows for greater vegetation growth and a variety of grazing animals to thrive. Zebras, wildebeests, and impalas roam the open areas, while giraffes and elephants stay closer to the trees for food and cover. Along with this abundance of prey, the area also boasts many predators like lions and leopards, and, where there is enough water, Nile crocodiles.

I was extremely fortunate on my African safari that our crew came face-to-face with numerous iconic animals I've been in awe of my entire life.

Here is a list of some of the amazing animals you may encounter roaming the open savanna:

Mammals: African elephants, Giraffes, Lions, Wildebeests, Cheetahs, Honey badgers, Impalas, Hippopotamuses, Servals
Reptiles: Leopard tortoises, Black mambas, African rock pythons, Nile monitor lizards
Birds: African gray hornbills, Secretary birds
Insects: Addo dung beetles

Wildebeest

Giraffes have extra-long necks and extra-long tongues for eating leaves off trees.

Giraffe

Cheetah

Nile monitor lizard

Nile monitor lizards can run, climb, or swim to hunt down prey.

African elephant

Elephants will flare their ears and stomp the ground when they are agitated.

When it's time to get out and explore, you'll need hiking boots and a backpack filled with:

- Binoculars
- A shade hat
- Sunscreen
- A bandana
- A camera with long lens
- Plenty of water!

Tranquilizers allowed us to get a close look at this lion's teeth. Whoa!

Lion

Addo dung beetle

Superior SURVIVAL Skills

Check out some of the character traits and tactics that help these species survive in the extreme savanna environment.

Wildebeest — strong horns for territorial disputes

Cheetah — a rudder-like tail to help with balance, supreme speed

African elephant — Super-strong and flexible trunk

Addo dung beetle — an insect strong enough to push ten times its weight

Hippopotomaus — powerful jaws and enormous tusklike teeth

Secretary bird — extra-long, extra-strong legs

Black mamba — one of the fastest snakes in Africa

Match the African animal to its survival skill.

This animal's venom could kill a human in fifteen minutes, but it much prefers bush squirrels for dinner.

This animal has the multi-tool of noses! This nose can lift; it can drink; it can trumpet! Plus, the nerve endings in the end of this nose can sense "underground" messages or vibrations from herd members miles away.

This animal's legs might be long and skinny, but they have a kick that can knock out a snake...and then the snake becomes supper. This fine feathered friend is fierce!

This animal gets its name from one of its primary food sources—other animals' waste/poop/manure/feces/droppings.

This animal looks tough, but it does not have thick skin, so it stays in the water all day to protect it from the sun. Luckily, the animal's eyes, ears, and nostrils are at the top of its head, so they remain out of the water and the animal remains alert.

This animal can run in short bursts at speeds over sixty miles per hour, which allows it catch its favorite prey, antelope.

This ungulate—hoofed animal—grazes in the open savanna in herds of up to 500 members and follows a migration cycle of over 1,500 miles per year!

The MANE Attraction

Find the highlighted words to complete this LION word search and improve your knowledge of Africa's most famous predator. Look forward, backward, up, down, and diagonally!

Lions live in the SAVANNA and hunt during both day and night, depending on when food is available

Lions are great cats, which means they ROAR, but do not purr. A lion's roar is loud and can be heard up to five miles away!

Only male lions have a MANE. Its purpose is to attract females, help the lion look larger and more intimidating, as well as protecting it during territorial disputes with other lions.

Lions are the only cat species to live in a group, called a PRIDE. A pride ranges from three to forty lions and consists of up to three males, several females, and their CUBS.

A female is called a LIONESS. They are the primary hunters for their pride. Their prey is usually faster and larger than they are, so TEAMWORK is necessary.

Lions are "apex PREDATORS," meaning they hunt other animals, but nothing hunts them.

Lions often hunt ZEBRAS, WILDEBEESTS, and BUFFALO.

Male lions protect the pride by guarding their TERRITORY, which can range up to 100 square miles!

Y	R	O	T	I	R	R	E	T	P	O	Z	W	Y	U
D	U	O	X	A	Q	T	R	R	L	G	U	I	B	N
M	Y	B	G	L	Z	U	E	A	X	A	U	L	X	Y
A	W	U	M	Y	L	D	F	A	E	C	P	D	B	X
K	U	B	E	A	A	F	B	P	V	S	L	E	K	W
Q	R	B	Y	T	U	J	P	T	W	A	Q	B	Q	S
L	Y	O	O	B	Z	E	B	R	A	S	R	E	G	S
H	R	R	W	O	C	T	W	K	I	O	Q	E	R	E
B	S	N	Y	M	E	N	A	M	A	D	P	S	E	N
Q	Q	A	D	M	A	A	C	R	R	A	E	T	T	O
L	P	K	V	P	Z	E	W	U	F	L	O	S	T	I
Z	D	Z	B	A	F	K	T	A	O	E	F	Z	U	L
J	Y	U	M	B	N	E	Z	F	Y	D	F	Y	I	H
Z	S	B	U	C	K	N	U	G	R	N	I	T	B	A
D	T	E	P	V	P	A	A	M	N	B	Z	E	L	L

The savanna is a harsh and dangerous habitat that, while brutally unforgiving, is also astonishingly beautiful and home to some of the most magnificent species in the world. Across the horizon, you may see the long neck of a giraffe reaching high for fresh leaves, a serval leaping into the air to grab dinner, or a cloud of dust as a herd of impala races to escape a predator.

THE ARCTIC

The Arctic is one of the coldest places on Earth—literally. During winter, temperatures often dip below -40 degrees Fahrenheit. *Brrrrr!* Snow and ice remain all year long this far north. Summer lasts only a few short weeks, bringing warmer temperatures and almost constant daylight. Most arctic animals use this opportunity to feast and build up fat reserves, as winter can be unbelievably long and brutal.

The animals here are incredibly well equipped for the frigid temperatures. Mammals have frost-proof, dense fur and thick layers of fat for protection, while birds have extra layers of down feathers to keep them warm. No matter how well adapted you are to the Arctic, it's a hard place to call home.

Here are some of the toughest arctic animals:

Mammals: Polar bears, Ringed seals, Musk ox, Arctic foxes, Caribous, Walruses, Narwhals
Birds: Little auk, Arctic terns, Puffins, Snowy owls

Polar bear

Polar bears are the largest carnivores living on land and mainly feed on seals.

Arctic tern

Puffin

DID YOU KNOW?

Puffins mate for life! Every summer, a flock gathers in the Arctic and lays eggs, and every winter, they migrate south!

Musk ox

This is the winter coat of the arctic fox. Their summer coats are brown!

Arctic fox

The term *reindeer* refers to domesticated caribou. All reindeer are caribou, but not all caribou are reindeer.

Caribou

Ringed seal

Here are Necessary Arctic Accessories:

- Winter jacket
- Beanie
- Ski goggles
- Winter gloves
- Winter boots
- Binoculars
- Camera with long lens
- Thermos with hot cocoa

These animals have all the best ARCTIC Adaptations!

Snowy owl

Heavy layers of feathers

Feather-covered legs

Puffin

They share a lot of superb physical traits that protect them from the dry, frigid artic conditions:

Short ears, snouts, and legs make an animal's body more compact, which keeps heat closer to their core.

Dark or black skin allows the animal to absorb the heat of the sun's rays.

Multiple layers of fur or feathers insulate the animal's body. The outer layer is made of coarse "guard" hairs that deflect piercing winds, while the waterproof inner layer provides warmth and insulation.

Feet padded with fur stay warmer, are less slippery, and spread out to distribute the animal's weight while walking on snow and ice.

Layers of feathers are great insulation—think of a down coat!

Arctic Hare

Short ears
Thick furry coat
Padded feet
Broad back legs

Arctic Fox

Short ears
Short muzzle
Two layers of fur
Padded feet

Caribou

Two layers of fur
Hooves have four wide toes and act like snowshoes

Polar Bear

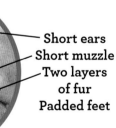

Two layers of fur
Blubber
Black skin
Padded paws

It helps to have BLUBBER!

Blubber (thick fat) is an extra-special adaptation accumulated only by mammals living in sub-zero temperatures, like seals, polar bears, and whales.

Brave the Arctic Blast:

Are the followig true or false? Circle your answer.

1 Blubber is an adaptation for animals that live lazy lifestyles.

True **or** False

2 Blubber on large mammals can be several feet thick.

True **or** False

3 Blubber is very heavy and causes sea-dwelling animals to sink.

True **or** False

FUN FACTS!

- Blubber insulates the body by trapping warmth inside.
- It adds buoyancy, which means it helps the animals float.
- It provides an extra energy source when food is scarce.

Taking off with an Artic Tern!

Can you follow the tern's path to see its route for migration?

ARCTIC

DID YOU KNOW?

The Arctic tern holds the record for the longest animal migration! Terns only stay in the arctic for summer, while raising their chicks. For winter, they fly all the way south to the islands near Antarctica. That's a total distance of nearly 20,000 miles every year!

ANTARCTIC

The Arctic is a breathtaking expanse of ice-blue water, blinding white snow, and jagged, monstrous mountains. When observing the Arctic ocean, you might catch a glimpse of a narwhal's twisted horn, the round body of a seal, or the *splash!* of a diving puffin. On land, a hare might whizz by, closely followed by a fox, each barely detectable against the white snow. Make sure you're bundled up; you won't want to miss the thrill of the arctic!

ANSWER KEY

Page 7:

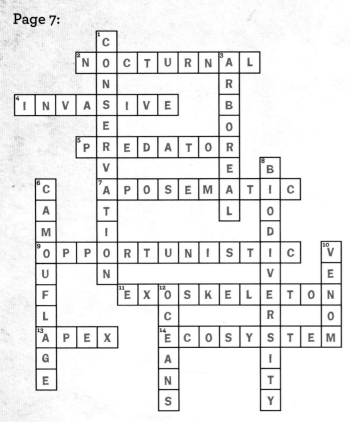

Crossword answers:
- 1. CONSERVATION (down)
- 2. NOCTURNAL
- 3. ARBOREAL (down)
- 4. INVASIVE
- 5. PREDATOR
- 6. CAMOUFLAGE (down)
- 7. APOSEMATIC
- 8. BODY (BIODIVERSITY down)
- 9. OPPORTUNISTIC
- 10. VENOMOUS (down)
- 11. EXOSKELETON
- 12. OCEANS (down)
- 13. APEX
- 14. ECOSYSTEM

Page 10:

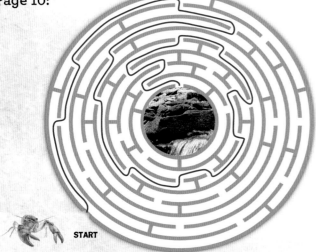

START

Page 11: C.1, E.2, D.3, A.4, B.5

Page 17: Both; Wolverine; Pine marten; Pine marten; Wolverine; Pine marten; Both; Both

Page 22: Kit fox (both); Tarantula hawk (Diurnal); Banded gecko (Nocturnal); Elf owl (Nocturnal); Collared lizard (Diurnal); Gila monster (Diurnal); Coyote (both); Roadrunner (Diurnal); Kangaroo rat (Nocturnal); Mexican free-tailed bat (Nocturnal)

Page 23:

Make a Match

Place the correct desert animal sticker with its name. Can you match them all without looking them up? Do your best!

- Regal horned lizard
- Desert blonde tarantula
- Giant desert hairy scorpion
- Roadrunner
- Kangaroo rat
- Desert tortoise
- Desert pocket mouse
- Western banded gecko
- Mexican free-tailed bat

Page 28: 1. Hiding in the Mud, Stinky musk, Aggressive chomp; 2. False; 3. For territory, For mates, For food; 4. Bask in the Sun, Lay eggs, Find another pond

Page 29: predators, mammals, fish, teeth, regenerate, aquatic, nostrils, tails, twenty, eggs, three, years, fifteen, pounds

Page 34-35: 1. Sea cucumber; 2. Ghost crab; 3. Banded sea urchin; 4. Moray eel; 5. Crown-of-thorns; 6. Scorpionfish; 7. Box jellyfish; 8. Textile cone snail; 9. Yellow-bellied sea snake

Page 41:

Page 52:

Page 53:

Page 59: 1. False; 2. True; 3. False

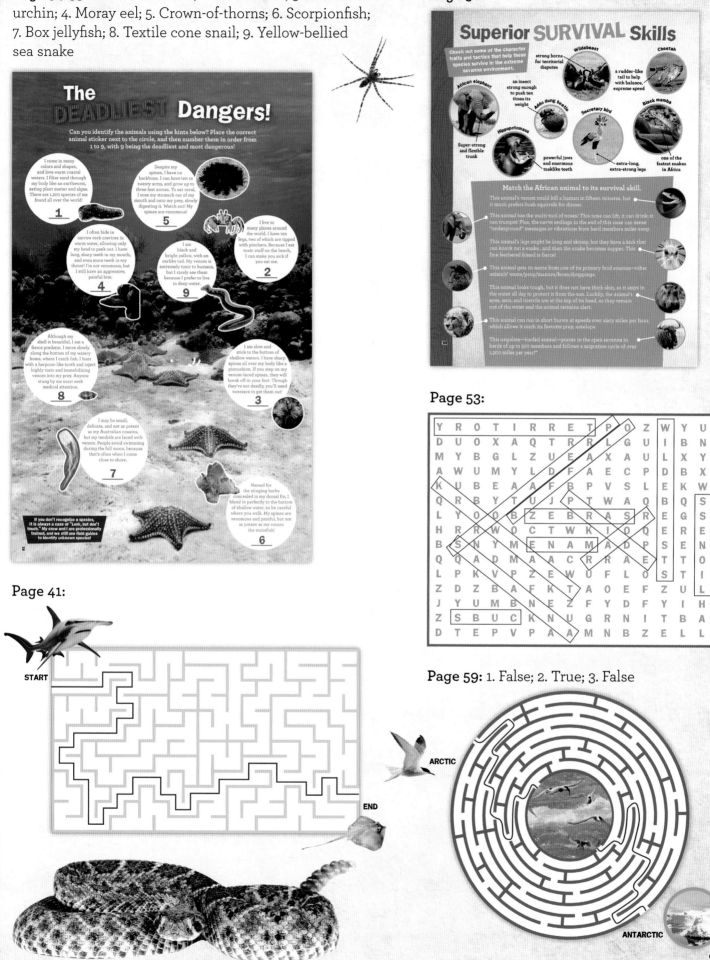

Little, Brown and Company
Hachette Book Group
1290 Avenue of the Americas, New York, NY 10104
Visit us at LBYR.com
bravewilderness.com

First Edition: November 2019

Little, Brown and Company is a division of Hachette Book Group, Inc.
The Little, Brown name and logo are trademarks of Hachette Book Group, Inc.

The publisher is not responsible for websites
(or their content) that are not owned by the publisher.

ISBN: 978-0-316-45804-7

Printed in CHINA

APS

10 9 8 7 6 5 4 3 2 1

Disclaimer: Coyote Peterson and the crew are professionally trained and receive assistance from animal experts when in potentially life-threatening situations. Never approach or attempt to handle wildlife on your own.